Musical Instruments

Recorder

By Nick Rebman

level
1
little blue
readers

www.littlebluehousebooks.com

Little Blue House is distributed by North Star Editions:
sales@northstareditions.com | 888-417-0195

Produced for Little Blue House by Red Line Editorial.

Photographs ©: Shutterstock Images, cover, 4, 7, 8–9, 13, 15, 16–17, 19, 21, 24 (top left), 24 (top right), 24 (bottom left), 24 (bottom right); iStockphoto, 11, 23

Library of Congress Control Number: 2022910601

ISBN
978-1-64619-701-9 (hardcover)
978-1-64619-733-0 (paperback)
978-1-64619-794-1 (ebook pdf)
978-1-64619-765-1 (hosted ebook)

Printed in the United States of America
Mankato, MN
012023

About the Author

Nick Rebman is a writer and editor who lives in Minnesota. He enjoys reading, walking his dog, and playing rock songs on his drum set.

Table of Contents

My Recorder

I have a recorder.

I can play music.

I have a recorder.

I blow into it.

I have a recorder.

I cover the holes.

hole

I have a recorder.

I make different sounds.

I have a recorder.

I play outside.

I have a recorder.

I play inside.

I have a recorder.

My teacher helps me.

I have a recorder.

I get better and better.

I have a recorder.

I play at school.

I have a recorder.

I play with a friend.

Glossary

friend

school

outside

teacher

Index